Interior Design Decoded

Building Your Business Empire

Table of Contents

Chapter 1. Introduction

Unveil the secrets of success in the realm of interior design with our Special Report: "Interior Design Decoded: Building Your Business Empire"! Let its pages inspire you, as they unlock the mysteries of building a compelling career in this dynamic field, painting an irresistible portrait of entrepreneurial prowess. Through vibrant storytelling, fierce industry insights and countless success stories, this guide will keep you reading, learning, and on the edge of your seat, eager for the wealth of exceptional wisdom yet to come. Say goodbye to uncertainty and hello to a future filled with creativity, passion and prosperity. Get your hands on this transformative treasure trove today – because to conquer the empire, you need to master the art!

Chapter 2. Unraveling the Fabric of Interior Design: An Introduction

When discussing interior design, understanding its essence is an intellectual necessity. Design, at its core, isn't just about crafting aesthetically pleasing spaces, it's also centered on incorporating utility, safety, and individuality. It is a timeless art form with a pulse on antecedent aesthetic epochs while also looking forward to future design trends. Defining the nuts and bolts, exploring its expansive canvas, and decrypting its influence on our daily lives is the starting point to mastering this empire of creative indulgence.

2.1. Primordial Beginnings of Interior Design

To comprehend interior design, we must first traverse back in time to its origins. The intrinsic human urge to decorate their surroundings can be traced back to the earliest cave paintings. From the need for shelter arose the desire for comfort, a sense of identity, and an expression of individual aesthetic leanings. Paintings, pottery, and sculpted figurines found in archaeological sites are testament to the fact that design was intertwined with human life from the very beginning.

2.2. The Evolution of Style and Space

Over the centuries, interior design has evolved, borrowing styles and influences from different timelines and cultures. The ancient Egyptians had a distinct architecture style that demonstrated their beliefs and their lifestyle. Renaissance architecture adopted symmetry, proportion, and geometry to create visually striking spaces.

Interior design as a formal discipline, however, was recognized only in the 20th century. The rise of industry, combined with an urbanized society and scientific advancements, sparked the conception of interior design as a specialized craft.

2.3. Functionality and Aesthetics: The Twin Pillars

To grasp the spirit of interior design, it's important to understand its two fundamental aspects: functionality and aesthetics. The former deals with the practical usage of a space, considering aspects like lighting, space utilization, and furnishings. The latter is concerned with creating visually captivating environments that evoke emotional responses and appreciations.

2.4. Decoding Elements and Principles of Design

Designers employ a suite of design elements, such as lines, color, shape, texture and light, to create a unique visual language. Understanding each of these elements is key to creating a space that is balanced and harmonious.

Another layer of complexity comes from principles that guide the use of these elements in design: balance, rhythm, emphasis, scale, and proportion. Mastering the interplay of these elements and principles allows one to create spaces that are both functional and appealing.

2.5. Design Styles: Personal Palates and Cultural Influences

Over the years, various design styles have emerged, bearing the imprint of different eras and cultures. These styles translate into unique design identities, from the ornate detailing of Georgian design, the simple elegance of Minimalism, to the classic charm of the Mid-Century Modern style.

Understanding these styles, their origins, nuances, and how to blend them is critical to acing interior design. Though styles might have predefined rules, innovative thinking could lead to the birth of hybrid styles, challenging the orthodox and adding a fresh perspective to design.

=== Client-Designer Synergy: Engaging with Clients

In the world of interior design, establishing a rapport with clients is intrinsic to success. A designer's role is to help translate the client's visions into reality. This requires exceptional communication skills, empathy, and a mighty dollop of patience. Understanding a client's needs, researching their style preferences, and creating designs that reflect their personality are crucial aspects of this art form.

2.6. Technology and Interior Design

With the digital revolution, the design industry has seen a sea-change. Modern technologies like VR and AR, 3D printing, graphic design software, and digital mood boards are transforming how designers work, adding precision, speed, and flexibility to their processes.

2.7. The Business of Interior Design

Equally important to mastering the art of interior design is understanding the economics behind it. From pricing and contracts, marketing and branding, project management to negotiating skills, grasping these nitty-gritties can spell the difference between thriving and surviving in this industry.

As we unravel the fabric of interior design, we begin to appreciate its multifaceted nature. This realm is not merely about decorating a space. It's about creating emotions, experiences, and environments that are reflective of people's persona, their dreams, and aspirations. As you embark on this journey into the labyrinth of interior design, remember that every turn, every corner has a tale to tell – a tale of human creativity, of personal narratives, and of spaces that are crafted to resonate with the soul.

Chapter 3. Business Planning: Setting a Solid Foundation

Setting a foundation for your interior design business is the keystone to your success. It involves the conception of your business model, the creation of your business plan, and an understanding of the marketing environment.

3.1. Understanding Your Business Model

Inherent in starting any business is an understanding of the business model. In essence, what do you offer? Who are your customers? How do your operations work, and how do you create value for your clientele?

Begin by determining what services you will offer. Will you take on full residential projects, from renovations to furniture selection and color scheme development, or will you specialize in a specific aspect of interior design?

Next, clearly outline your target audience. This might be based on location, budget, property type, or personal style. By knowing your audience, you can better tailor your services and marketing strategy to their specific needs and wants.

Consider your operations too. Will you have a physical office, or will you operate remotely? Do you need employees, or can you manage all tasks yourself with the assistance of contractors or freelancers for specialized jobs?

Lastly, understand how your business creates value for its clients. You might distinguish your business through customized design solutions, exceptional customer service, or a unique aesthetic.

3.2. Crafting Your Business Plan

The next step in building a solid foundation is crafting your business plan. This detailed summary of your business operations, goals, and strategies serves as an operational guide for your business and an essential tool for communicating with potential investors and financial institutions.

Your business plan should include:

- A clear description of your business concept and value proposition.
- An overview of your services and products.
- A detailed understanding of your target audience.
- A competitive analysis.
- A marketing and sales plan.
- A financial forecast and funding requests.

Remember, an excellent business plan is adaptable, allowing you to pivot your strategies as your business environment changes.

3.3. Conducting a Market Analysis

Understanding your market environment is crucial for the overall success of your business. It helps you identify the key trends, understand the competition, and recognize the opportunities and threats facing you in the market. You should conduct a Strength, Weaknesses, Opportunities, and Threats (SWOT) analysis to assess both internal and external variables that could affect your business.

In conducting a market analysis, consider:

- The existing market size and potential for growth.

- Current trends and how they might impact your business in the future.

- Your primary competitors, their strengths, and weaknesses.

- The opportunities and threats present in the market.

3.4. Developing Your Market Strategy

Your market strategy outlines how you plan to reach your target audience, attract clients, and achieve a competitive edge in the market. This should encompass your brand identity, marketing initiatives, pricing strategy, and distribution channels.

Starting with your brand identity, determine your business's look, feel, and voice. This is crucial as it influences how your target audience perceives and interacts with your brand.

For marketing initiatives, consider a mix of traditional and digital marketing strategies. This could include networking events, collaborations with other businesses, social media marketing, email newsletters, blog posts, and search engine optimization.

When it comes to pricing, ensure your rates reflect the value you deliver and are competitive within the market while still providing profitability.

In deciding your distribution channels, consider whether your services will be available online, at a physical location, or both.

3.5. Setting Up Your Financial Plan

A financial plan is essential in managing your resources, attracting investors, and ensuring profitability. It should include profit and loss projections, cash flow forecasts, balance sheet projections, and a capital expenditure budget.

Remember, financial planning is not a one-time event but a continuous process as your business evolves. Regularly review and adjust your financial plan to reflect your current situation and future predictions.

Embarking on your entrepreneurial journey in interior design is thrilling and rewarding. By solidifying your business model, crafting a dynamic business plan, conducting a detailed market analysis, developing a well-rounded market strategy, and carefully planning your finances, you're setting a solid foundation that will drive your business towards success!

Chapter 4. Branding Brilliance: Creating Your Unique Identity

Building an identity in the interior design industry is like a room waiting to be filled with creativity, personality, and uniqueness. In a sea signified by competition, you need an artistic yet strategic touch for your brand to float and stand out. A dynamic, innovative, and planned branding strategy is like your bespoke blueprint for success.

4.1. Understanding Branding and its Importance

Branding is the process of identifying, creating, and managing your company's identity. It reflects your business's goals, values, strengths, and the unique elements you bring to the table. A well-established brand will form a connection with clients, building trust and often leading the charge in persuasion and decision-making.

In the realm of interior design, branding is particularly significant. With styles more diverse, clients more discerning, and competition ever-increasing, a robust brand identity can be your circuit breaker to stand out amidst the landscape.

For interior designers, their brand serves as an extension of their style and ethos. Whether minimalist or maximalist, Scandinavian or Bohemian, your brand connects the thousands of dots that speak volumes about your design language, professional beliefs, and business reputation.

4.2. Creating your Unique Identity: A Step-by-Step Process

Define your Brand Mission

Before you can build your brand, you need to understand what drives it. Your brand mission underlines what you aim to accomplish as a designer and brand. It succinctly encapsulates the essence of what you do and why you do it.

When crafting your brand mission, think about who your target clients are, how you want to impact them with your services, and what promises your brand can deliver consistently.

Develop your Brand Vision

After defining your mission, it's important to visualize the broader picture: your brand vision. This outlines where you aim to see your brand in the long-term.

Whether it is to be recognized as a leading global interior designer for luxury homes or the go-to brand for eco-friendly, sustainable office spaces, your brand vision will serve as your North Star, guiding your course of action and decisions to achieve the same.

Identify your Unique Selling Proposition (USP)

To stand out, it's essential you offer something distinct to your clients. Your USP is what makes your brand unique - it is something you do or provide that no other interior design brand can claim in the same way.

Maybe it is your distinctive design style, extensive experience with a particular type of project, or commitment to sustainability. Understanding your USP will not only differentiate you from your competitors but also provide a compelling reason for prospective clients to choose you.

Design a Stand-Out Logo and Tagline

Your logo is the visual cornerstone of your brand. It is one of the first things prospective clients will see, and consistently used across all your marketing collaterals and communications.

When designing your logo, consider elements that resonate with your brand identity – the style, color scheme, and font. Make it unique but also timeless.

Your tagline, much like your logo, is a concise representation of your brand promise. Keep it short, memorable, engaging, and make sure it aligns with your brand mission, vision, and values.

Create a Consistent Brand Message

Every piece of content or communication you put out there should resonate with your brand and its promise. From your website's content to your social media posts, consistency in your brand voice builds trust and enhances recognition.

Don't forget the importance of engaging visuals in your brand message, especially in an industry such as interior design. High-quality images of your work can be incredibly persuasive in winning over potential clients.

4.3. Mastering the Art of Brand Storytelling

Storytelling is an integral part of branding. To create an emotional connection with your audience, do not just tell them what you do; show them why you do it.

Your brand story isn't a marketing campaign; it's a compass that provides direction and purpose to your branding efforts. It reflects your journey, your values, the challenges you've overcome, and the achievements you've earned.

When it comes to conveying your brand story, authenticity and transparency weigh gold. They help build credibility and trust among your target audience, making your brand more relatable and convincing.

4.4. Connecting it all: Cohesion and Consistency

From your website to your social media platforms, from your business card to your e-mail signature, every touchpoint should reflect your brand identity – consistent, cohesive, and unmistakable.

Consistency goes beyond repeated application. It entails employing the same tone, visuals, messaging across different platforms and mediums. This way, your brand remains recognizable, inevitably strengthening trust and awareness over time.

Branding, despite its challenges, can shape the trajectory of your career in interior design. By leveraging a well-thought-out strategy, you not only carve a unique brand but create an omnipresent voice that rings loud in clients' minds, echoes across the industry, leaving an indelible imprint. Layout a solid foundation for your brand, then let it evolve, mature, and get etched in the annals of the design empire. Remember, you are not just designing spaces; you're crafting experiences, one brand story at a time.

Chapter 5. Marketing Strategies: Showcase Your Expertise

How do you carve out a space for yourself in this fiercely competitive world of interior design? How do you display the expanse of your creative talent to potential clients and investors? The answer is simple: through strategic marketing.

To establish an effective marketing strategy, there are several critical components: identifying your target audience, honing a unique value proposition, utilizing digital channels, developing strong client relationships, and finally, measuring your success.

5.1. Define your target audience

Determine your design aesthetic and the clientele that will be most drawn to your elements of style. Craft a customer persona describing your ideal client – their age, occupation, salary, lifestyle, and tastes. This will serve as a guide in every marketing decision and naturally attract those who will appreciate your work the most.

5.2. Develop a unique value proposition

Identifying what sets you apart from your competitors is a crucial task. Is it your design aesthetic, project management skills, or sustainable practices? Emphasizing these unique aspects will make your business stand out in the crowded market. Your unique value proposition (UVP) should always transpire in your marketing materials and communications, painting a picture of why a client should choose you over another designer.

5.3. Utilize digital marketing channels

With today's advancements in technology, you have the world at your fingertips. Your online presence is paramount to your success. Get to know the different digital marketing channels and utilise them effectively:

- A compelling website: Your website is your online portfolio. It should be visually stunning, informative, and easy to navigate. Invest in good quality photographs of your work and provide potential clients with compelling descriptions.

- Social Media: Instagram, Pinterest, and Houzz are popular platforms for showcasing design portfolios. Engage with your audience by posting regularly and responding to comments.

- Online advertising: SEO, SEM, and PPC are great ways to increase visibility and gather potential leads.

- Content Marketing: Write about trends, tutorials, and case studies. Show your expertise and passion for the field.

5.4. Cultivate strong relationships

Creating strong relationships with clients, partners, and industry colleagues is key to establishing a well-regarded reputation and driving word-of-mouth referrals.

- Client relationships: Request client feedback after projects, and make it a habit to follow up. Holding onto client relationships can lead to repeat business and referrals.

- Vendor partnerships: Regular communication and fair treatment of your vendors will boost your reputation, and vendors may even become an unexpected source of referrals.

- Industry networking: Attend industry events and join online discussion groups. Collaborative relationships with other designers can help with resource sharing and professional growth.

5.5. Measure your success

In order to improve, you need to measure. Identify the key metrics for each channel. Look at website visits, bounce rates, and conversions for your website. Followers, shares, likes, and comments for your social media. Track these metrics, see the patterns, and adjust your strategy as needed.

Remember, success isn't overnight. It requires persistent effort, constant learning, and strategic planning. Don't be afraid to take risks and push the boundaries of your creativity. Your unique voice has a place in the interior design industry, and strategic marketing will help establish it. So, start planning, strategizing, and conquering your marketing efforts today!

Chapter 6. Networking: Building Strong Connections in the Industry

Major shifts, both technological and economic, have resulted in a dynamic business landscape for interior designers. True growth requires strategic thinking and a keen understanding of where your connections can lead you. Networking has evolved to be one of the vital keys to success in this industry, and understanding its strategies and techniques can catapult your business venture into the realm of the remarkable.

6.1. The Art of Building Relationships

The art of networking is more about building relationships than making transactions. Relationships form the foundation of trust and credibility, bonding you with others in the industry, and potentially resulting in mutual benefits down the line.

It's crucial to foster these relationships long before you will need their assistance. However, remember to be genuine in your interaction, rather than focusing solely on potential outcomes. Genuine interactions can yield synergy, a powerful tool for collective industry problem-solving and creating innovative and unique designs. You must network not only outwardly to potential clients but also to fellow designers, suppliers, and contractors.

6.2. Maximizing Social Events

Often overlooked as a networking platform, social events and parties can be a gateway to forming important industry connections. From trade shows to design conferences, these events are magnificent hotspots brimming with potential contacts.

Creating a strong impression is essential. Be sure to dress appropriately, present yourself confidently, carry business cards, and be prepared with a brief introduction of yourself and your business. Engage in meaningful conversations, showing genuine interest in others' work, as this helps form bonds that could foster future partnerships or business opportunities.

Remember, you are a representation of your business. Everything you do, say, and how you present yourself will reflect back on your business. So, ensure you represent it well.

6.3. Making Use of Online Platforms

In the digital age, it's impossible to ignore the profound impact of online platforms on networking. Social media outlets such as LinkedIn, Instagram, Facebook, and Twitter have revolutionized how we establish and maintain relationships. Harness the power of these tools and use them to your advantage.

LinkedIn can be an excellent tool for acquiring contacts in your field. It allows you to share updates about your business, build an online presence, and connect with like-minded professionals. Instagram, with its visual focus, is a perfect platform for displaying your work. Sharing past projects, ongoing work, and inspiration pieces can attract clients and fellow designers with whom you can collaborate. Learn to use these platforms effectively, posting regularly, and maintaining a cohesive brand image.

However, remember digital networking doesn't replace the value of face-to-face communication. It should supplement in-person networking, not substitute it.

6.4. Networking Organizations and Associations

Joining professional organizations and associations can extend your network significantly. Such organizations provide excellent opportunities for meeting industry influencers, potential partners, and mentors. They also frequently organize seminars and workshops that help you upskill while simultaneously extending your network.

Organizations like the American Society of Interior Designers (ASID), the International Interior Design Association (IIDA), and other locally centered organizations should be on your radar. They often provide benefits including listings in directories, subscriptions to newsletters, invitations to events, and exclusive resources, all of which serve the shared aim of fostering a vibrant design community.

6.5. The Role of Mentorship

In any industry, having a mentor can be invaluable. Within the interior design field, mentors can guide you through the intricacies of the business, provide industry insights that are difficult for beginners to grasp, and help you identify your own strengths and weaknesses.

A mentor is usually a seasoned professional who has profound knowledge and experience in the field. Apart from entrepreneurial advice, they can provide constructive criticism of your work, introduce you to key connections in their network and potentially accelerate your career trajectory.

Networking is as much about giving as it is about receiving. As you advance in your career, consider becoming a mentor. Guiding newcomers in the industry strengthens the community you're part of and cements your reputation as an industry leader.

6.6. The Power of Collaboration

Working with other professionals can be an incredible networking and learning platform and can expand your range of expertise. Collaborations introduce you to new methods, perspectives, and enhance your own skills.

Joint projects, whether they're with other interior designers, architects, or artists, can raise your profile and draw in a wider audience for your work. They also give you a chance to share industry knowledge and contacts, strengthening your position in the interior design landscape.

6.7. Remember, Networking is a Long-Term Investment

Much like designing, networking is an ongoing, organic process. A relationship built today may open a door years into the future, and connections evolve over time. Networking is not about immediate gratification but the potential for long-term professional opportunities.

Do not underestimate the power of a strong network. Carefully nurture your relationships, both online and offline, as these connections could lead to future clients, partnerships, or even mentorships. In an increasingly competitive environment, networking has the ability to set your interior design business apart and see it thrive.

Keep your eyes open for networking opportunities, and remember that each person you meet could potentially become a contact that will aid in your success. So go out there and start building your empire, one connection at a time!

Chapter 7. Financial Mastery: Pricing, Profit Margins and More

The path to financial success in the dynamic world of interior design is paved with strategic pricing, accurate profit margins, optimized overhead costs, and efficient financial management. Getting a firmer grip on these concepts can help turn your passion for designing beautiful spaces into a profitable enterprise.

7.1. Understanding Your Costs

The cornerstone of pricing your interior design services lies in understanding your costs. While each project is unique, they all share common cost components that need consideration.

1. Labor Cost: This is the time that you and your staff spend on a project. You would need to decide on an hourly rate that factors in your expertise, the quality of your work, your geographical location, and market competition.

2. Material Cost: This is where the costs of paint, furniture, art, decoration and other materials are accounted for. It is crucial to keep track of these costs meticulously.

3. Overhead Cost: These are ongoing costs that keep your business running, such as rent or mortgage for your workspace, utilities, insurance, advertising, and software.

4. Profit Margin: This is the percentage of the total project cost that you add above your combined labor, material, and overhead costs to determine your final pricing.

7.2. Creating a Pricing Strategy

A well-crafted pricing strategy is the heart of a profitable interior design business. There are several strategies you can consider.

1. Cost-Plus Pricing: In this strategy, you add a profit percentage to your costs. This strategy's strength lies in its simplicity and transparency and is most effective when you have a clear understanding of all the costs associated with a project.

2. Fixed Pricing: Here, you charge a fixed price for your services regardless of the effort or time involved. This strategy is most suited when you have a clear understanding of the project's scope and can accurately estimate the effort needed.

3. Hourly Pricing: In this approach, you charge a specific rate for every hour that you work on the project. This strategy is most effective when project timelines fluctuate, or the client's requirements are unclear or expected to change.

7.3. Tracking Profit Margins

Profit margins provide a clear perspective on the profitability of your business or a specific project. The basic formula to calculate your profit margin is (Total Revenue - Total Cost) / Total Revenue. It's important to study this number and understand what it means in terms of your business profitability.

1. Gross Profit Margin: This is the profit margin for a specific project calculated by subtracting the cost of labor and materials from the revenue and dividing by the total revenue.

2. Net Profit Margin: This is the profit margin for your entire business determined by subtracting all costs (including overheads) from your revenue and dividing by total revenue.

3. Ideal Profit Margin: There is no one-size-fits-all answer to what

your profit margin should be. By tracking your margins over time, you can identify profitable and unprofitable projects, adjust your pricing, manage your cost better, and make informed business decisions.

7.4. Negotiating With Vendors

Successful negotiation with vendors can help you reduce your material costs and increase your profit margins. It's important to build strong relationships with your vendors, understand their pricing models and terms, and use your negotiation skills to secure the best prices.

7.5. Overseeing Financial Management

Effective financial management is critical for the continued success of your interior design business. Using financial management software can help you to track your costs, manage your bills and invoices, monitor your profit margins, and keep your finances organized.

In conclusion, mastering the financial aspects of your business needs a strategic approach. By understanding your costs, developing a strong pricing strategy, tracking your profit margins, building robust vendor relationships, and overseeing efficient financial management, you can step confidently into a future of prosperity. Remember, it's not just about creating beautiful designs; it's also about creating a robust, financially-healthy business!

Chapter 8. Showcasing Success: Crafting an Irresistible Portfolio

In every interior designer's journey, there stands one crucial component that can open doors leading to breathtaking opportunities—the portfolio. A well-structured, expressively designed, and meticulously curated portfolio acts as a beacon, offering a kaleidoscope view into the designer's skills, vision, and creativity. Crafted and displayed wisely, a portfolio can become the golden ticket to building manifold connections, securing high-profile projects, and rising up the ranks in the competitive field of interior design.

8.1. The Fundamentals: What to Include

An interior design portfolio is not just a random collection of images or a quaint showcase of your work. It's a visual testament to your personal style, skill, and experience. A singular representation of your journey through and understanding of design.

Every project successfully completed, every design challenge conquered adds to your unique tapestry of skills. Yet, within your portfolio, not all projects are created equal. A good rule of thumb is to exhibit between eight to twelve of your best projects, where your clear understanding of design rules and creative prowess shine alongside your ability to shape a space. A well-composed blend of projects will illustrate your versatility and adaptability within different design aesthetics.

At its core, your portfolio should display exceptional high-resolution photographs of your work. This is where attention to detail becomes vital. Complement these images with brief narratives describing each project, the brief you worked with, the challenges you faced, the solutions you conjured, and the ultimate outcome. By doing this, you're not only showcasing your design skills but also your problem-solving prowess and your command over visual storytelling.

8.2. A Picture Paints a Thousand Words: Ideal Project Photography

The quality of photographs portrays the level of commitment toward your work. Blurry, poorly-lit images would not only be an injustice to your designs but also depreciate the overall appearance of your portfolio.

The best way to ensure exemplary project photography is to hire a professional photographer with experience in interior design photography. Good photographers efficiently capture the essence of your design, focusing on the details and overall mood, and bring it to the forefront in the images. Ensure that the photographs cover overall room views as well as close shots of specific elements, features, or details that you want to highlight.

When selecting images, choose the ones that tell the story of your project best – from before photos, if applicable, to the process and the end result. Show the journey, the progress, the transformation. This will add depth and context to your work, allowing potential clients or employers to appreciate your ability to bring about marked change in a space.

8.3. Piecing the Puzzle: Structuring Your Portfolio

The portfolio's structure plays an integral role in its effectiveness and impact. Start strong. Make your first project a knockout, showcasing your best work. This meeting of incredible project and excellent photography will create a lasting first impression.

Next, vary the content throughout. If your first project sports minimalistic design, make your second one more vibrant and complex. The aim is to strike a balance to keep your readers interested and engaged all the way through.

Lastly, end on a high note. The portfolio's final showcase should be equally as impressive as the first, leaving the viewer longing for more. This helps to capture their interest and leaves a lasting impression.

In terms of layout, keep it clean and easy to navigate. Select a straightforward and professional template that allows your work to shine without unnecessary distractions. Remember, less is often more when it comes to design.

8.4. Textual Telling: Writing About Your Work

While images may be the limelight of your portfolio, never underestimate the importance of accompanying text—your words structure your visual narrative and deepen the viewer's understanding of your designs.

For each project, start with an enticing title that summarizes its essence. Follow this with a short, engaging introduction. Dig deeper by describing the design process–your planning pathway, challenges faced, and solutions designed. To round it off, provide a succinct summary of the outcome and impacts of your design.

Inject your personal voice into your portfolio by writing in the first person, enabling potential clients or employers to sense your passion for design and your determination to solve design challenges.

8.5. The Virtual Visage: Crafting Your Online Portfolio

In the current digital age, having a compelling online portfolio is no longer an optional extra—it's a necessity. A searchable online portfolio can help you reach out to a wider audience, expand your client base, and land incredible opportunities.

When designing your online portfolio, user experience should be at the fore. A website that is easy to navigate, with clear menus and categories, aids potential clients or employers to explore your work effortlessly. Providing an about section outlining your professional background and achievements, a contact page, and links to your social media channels adds to this experience.

In conclusion, the art of creating an effective interior design portfolio lies in carefully selecting, presenting, and describing your work. Like an artist meticulous about his masterpiece, take the time to craft your portfolio with precision. Let your creativity and innovation spark interest, leading to new opportunities and the growth of your interior design business.

Chapter 9. The Role of Technology: Harnessing the Digital Age

From the advent of computers to the ubiquity of smartphones, technology has revolutionized the global landscape. In the realm of interior design, the digital age has ushered in an era of unforeseen opportunities and tools that have reconfigured the form and function of business as we know it.

9.1. The Internet: A Repository of Inspiration

In the early days of interior design, professionals were predominantly reliant on print publications and books for inspiration and new ideas. Now, they have the internet—a vast, vibrant, and continuous stream of visual inspiration. E-platforms like Pinterest, Instagram, and Houzz deliver an endless supply of design ideas, trends, and visual concepts right to your fingertips. Nevertheless, it's essential to utilize these resources judiciously, understanding their place in the grand scheme of the design process.

Social networking sites have also provided a platform for showcasing work, building a brand, and enhancing a designer's visibility. An engaging online presence has become an integral element of effective marketing strategy among today's designers. Anyone with an internet connection now can view and appreciate your work. Gone are the days of circulating physical portfolios.

9.2. Digital Tools and Software

Beyond the internet, an array of digital tools and software have reshaped the industry. Tools like CAD (Computer-Aided Design) have revolutionized the design process, allowing designers to create, edit, and manipulate 3D models on a computer screen. This capability often allows clients to visualize a finished product before turning the first screw.

Systematic software programs like project management tools streamline the managerial aspect, offering better document organization, timeline tracking, and communication between the designer, client, and contractors. These tools play an essential role in executing tasks efficiently, keeping projects on track, and preventing any logistical nightmares.

Similarly, virtual and augmented reality technology has a tremendous impact. At one end of the spectrum, virtual reality can immerse clients in a fully realized 3D model of a proposed design; at the other end, augmented reality can overlay digital renderings onto the physical space via mobile devices. These immersive experiences significantly contribute to decision-making processes.

9.3. E-commerce and Online Sourcing

Perhaps one of the most significant shifts in the operation of design businesses has been the rise of e-commerce platforms. No longer limited to local retailers and showrooms, designers can now source materials, furniture, and accessories from international vendors, bringing the world to their clients' doorsteps.

Platforms like Wayfair, Alibaba, and Etsy have expanded design horizons, sparking creativity with their vast variety of products. Designers can broaden their scope and source unique items to create distinctive interior spaces. The cost-effectiveness and convenience of online shopping are undeniable advantages in sourcing and developing an ever-evolving aesthetic.

9.4. The Rise of DIY Design Tools

Do-it-yourself design platforms are another technological offshoot that has brought design capabilities to the masses. Software and online tools like Canva, Homestyler, and Sketchup enable anyone to design spaces, challenging the traditional role of interior designers.

In this new reality, the role of a professional interior designer has evolved— they must now provide something beyond what these digital platforms can offer. This provides an opportunity to reinforce the value of their expertise and create truly compelling narratives for their clients.

9.5. Adopting New Technologies: Challenges and Rewards

With every technological advancement comes a learning curve. Professional adaptation to new tools can be a significant investment of time and resources. Despite the initial challenges, however, the rewards of embracing technology far outweigh the costs. Larger audiences, streamlined processes, and enhanced visual communication are just a few of the benefits that digitization brings to the interior design industry.

Learning to harness the digital age is pivotal for success in today's interior design industry. This era of rapid technology innovation compels professionals to stay current and adaptable. As the role of technology continues to evolve, it is those designers who leverage these tools that will build empires in the industry.

Chapter 10. Safeguarding Your Enterprise: Understanding Legal and Ethical Dimensions

Navigating the terrain of interior design is not merely an endeavor of artistic creativity and business acumen; it's also a journey that requires meticulous attention to legal and ethical dimensions. Let us embark on a comprehensive exploration of these aspects, to ensure your enterprise stands on solid ethical and legal ground.

10.1. Comprehending Legal Foundations

The inception of any successful business starts with a thorough understanding of the legal foundations pertinent to the industry, and interior design is no different. Familiarizing yourself with the legal obligations can save you from potential disastrous lawsuits and financial losses.

10.1.1. Business Structure

Decisions on the structure of your business will influence every legal interaction you will have moving forward - from tax considerations to liabilities and succession plans. You need to choose whether to operate as a sole trader, partnership, limited liability company (LLC), or corporation. Reach out to legal consultants or regional authority entities to acquire the needed knowledge about the legal implications of each type of business entity.

10.1.2. Contracts

An impeccable contract is the backbone of any transaction in interior design. A contract should be comprehensive, elucidating rights, obligations, and the agreed-upon deliverables with lucidity. Everything from design proposals to provisions for unexpected changes or disputes should be covered in a carefully curated legal contract.

10.1.3. Intellectual Property

Every design you conceive is safeguarded by Intellectual Property (IP) laws, which include copyrights, patents, and trademarks. Recognizing these laws, and learning how to protect your creations through them, will ensure that your ideas cannot be stolen or replicated without your consent.

10.1.4. Legal Permits and Licenses

As with any business, you'll need to obtain the appropriate permits and licenses to operate legally. This may include a business license, sales tax license, or professional license, depending on your location. Be sure to research your local regulations and ensure all your legal paperwork is in order.

10.2. Walking the Ethical Path

Ethical considerations are overlooked sometimes, but they often play an instrumental role in achieving long-term success. Upholding ethical values means cultivating trust, which translates into repeat business and referrals.

10.2.1. Honesty and Transparency

While it may be tempting to promise clients the moon, it's important to provide realistic expectations. This can include factors such as costs, timelines, potential issues, and other aspects of your designs. Transparency is a key aspect in gaining, maintaining, and fostering trust between you and your clients.

10.2.2. Respect for Clients' Preferences

A significant virtue lies in meeting a cleint's design needs rather than imposing your vision. Your role is to bring your client's dream to life, and this should supersede any personal preferences. In every interaction, ensure you are serving their interests first, rather than your own.

10.2.3. Fair Competition

Ethical practices also extend to relationships with your competitors. This includes not disparaging their work or poaching their clients. Instead, foster a supportive community that propels the entire industry forward.

10.2.4. Social Responsibility

Today's consumer values businesses that operate responsibly, considering the impact of their operations on the environment and society. In your designs, consider embracing green practices, local sourcing, and sustainable materials.

In conclusion, understanding and aligning your enterprise with the legal and ethical dimensions of international design is not just a precaution; it's a cornerstone to the longevity and integrity of your business. By adhering to legal requirements and maintaining high ethical standards, you'll foster an environment of trust, integrity, and responsibility, which ultimately connects to the deeper essence of success.

Chapter 11. The Future Awaits: Scaling Your Empire

The future of business in the realm of interior design is as bright and glistening as a perfectly polished marble countertop. It's a canvas full of potential, a world rich with opportunities, and it's all yours for the taking. This journey onto the next stage of your empire building journey is set to be an exhilarating adventure.

11.1. Choosing Your Next Steps

The domain of interior design is expansive and moving upward requires strategic planning. Your actions at this stage should be careful, calculated, and committed to growth. Revisit your business plan at regular intervals, researching emerging market trends and identifying opportunities for improved efficiency and profitability. There is a wealth of data at your fingertips, and the insights you gain will be instrumental in driving your business upward.

11.2. Building A Robust Business Model

Deep, strategic thinking needs to be inspired by your business model. What has brought you success so far? How can you replicate and expand upon this success? Your business model should be robust and flexible enough to adapt to changing conditions in the market. Think outside the box: Could there be untapped areas in the scope of design services? Are there innovative solutions you could provide? Are there any geographical locations you haven't touched yet?

11.3. Fostering Your Team's Growth

An empire is not built alone. Your team, the people who make your vision come to life, need an environment that fosters growth. Prioritise leadership development, invest in ongoing learning and training, and create an environment that promotes creativity and innovation. Encourage collaboration and teamwork, empower your staff to make decisions, and reward exceptional performances. Equip your team with the tools and knowledge they need to drive your empire to new heights.

11.4. Leveraging Technology

Don't underestimate the power of technology in scaling your business. From project management tools to virtual reality design apps, embrace the digital revolution to improve productivity and customer experience. The integration of technology will not only streamline your operations but also provide an edge over your competitors.

11.5. Building Strong Relationships

A successful interior design business thrives on relationships - with clients, suppliers, stakeholders, and the community. Foster these relationships with transparency, professionalism, and a commitment to delivering exceptional quality. By meeting and exceeding client expectations, your brand will earn referrals, further expanding your growth potential.

11.6. Marketing Your Brand

No matter how exceptional your work, your empire will be limited without an effective marketing strategy. Through both traditional and digital marketing channels, amplify your brand voice, showcase your portfolio, and reach new audiences. A well-curated social media presence can immensely boost your reputation and reach, driving client engagements and business growth.

The journey to scaling your empire in the world of interior design has no definitive end, and that's the beauty of it. Your empire expands as you grow, pushing boundaries, shattering expectations, and surpassing your visions. And as you take each step forward, remember to enjoy the journey, for it is in the process of scaling that your empire becomes truly your own. Embrace each challenge as an opportunity and every setback as a learning experience. After all, at the heart of every successful empire is a leader who never stopped learning, innovating, and pushing beyond the horizon of possibilities.

11.7. The Final Word

Your future in interior design awaits, overflowing with the promise of creativity, passion and prosperity. And within this guide, you've gained the wisdom you need to navigate this mesmerizing journey ahead. You've learned, you've grown – now, all that's left is to leap forward, breaking barriers, and scaling your empire. Your toolkit is complete, your blueprint is in place, it's time to make your mark on the world of interior design.

Scaling your interior design empire is a journey of discovery and determination. It's about finding the equilibrium between creativity and technicality, between intuition and strategy. The balance between these elements is pivotal to your entrepreneurial prosperity and it's this balance that will ultimately set your empire apart. Forge ahead with an unwavering will, a clear vision, and an unquenchable passion – towards a future gleaming with opportunity, a future that awaits. Your empire awaits.

Remember, to conquer the empire, you indeed need to master the art! And mastering the art is a continuous journey. After all, the key to empire-building is in evolving with the times and staying ahead of the curve. It's time to seize control and scale new heights. Because, in the realm of interior design, the future really does wait.

www.ingramcontent.com/pod-product-compliance
Lightning Source LLC
Chambersburg PA
CBHW060858260726
48661CB00008B/3334